A DUFFER'S DICTIONARY

golfing

A DUFFER'S DICTIONARY

BY HENRY BEARD & ROY McKIE

Methuen

by the same authors

Gardening
Fishing
Cooking

A METHUEN PAPERBACK

Original edition first published in the United States of America in 1987
by Workman Publishing Company, New York

This revised edition first published in Great Britain in 1990 by
Methuen London, Michelin House, 81 Fulham Road, London SW3 6RB

Reprinted 1990

The authors have asserted their moral rights

ISBN 0 413 63530 9

A CIP catalogue record for this book is available from the British Library

Printed and bound in Great Britain by
St Edmundsbury Press Ltd, Bury St Edmunds, Suffolk

To those who have heard the call of the tee.

Addressing the Ball

A

Ace

Completion of a hole in a single stroke. The odds against this happening are about 45,000 to 1—somewhat worse than the odds of finding a brand-new ball lost in the rough (27,000 to 1) but considerably better than the odds of hitting a perfect drive off a crowded first tee (1,195,000 to 1). *See* HOLE-IN-ONE.

Addressing the Ball

1. Assuming the correct stance and placing the head of the club on the ground behind the ball prior to hitting it.
2. Directing statements to the ball before it is hit or while it is in flight, such as: "If you go into that trap, I'll never wash you again" or "In a way, I hope you miss that cup—I've always wondered what's inside a golf ball."

Advice

According to the rules of golf, advice is "any counsel or suggestion made by one golfer to another about the choice of club, method of play or making of a shot, which contains no more than five errors of fact, contradictory statements or harmful recommendations. Six or more such pieces of misinformation or misinstruction shall constitute a formal golf lesson."

Age Players

Accomplished golfers who have recorded one of two equally unusual golfing achievements: playing a round of 18 holes at the end of which they had a score equal to their age, or playing a round of 18 holes during all of which they acted their age.

All Square

A term used in match play to indicate that both teams or individuals have cheated on an equal number of holes. *See* DORMIE.

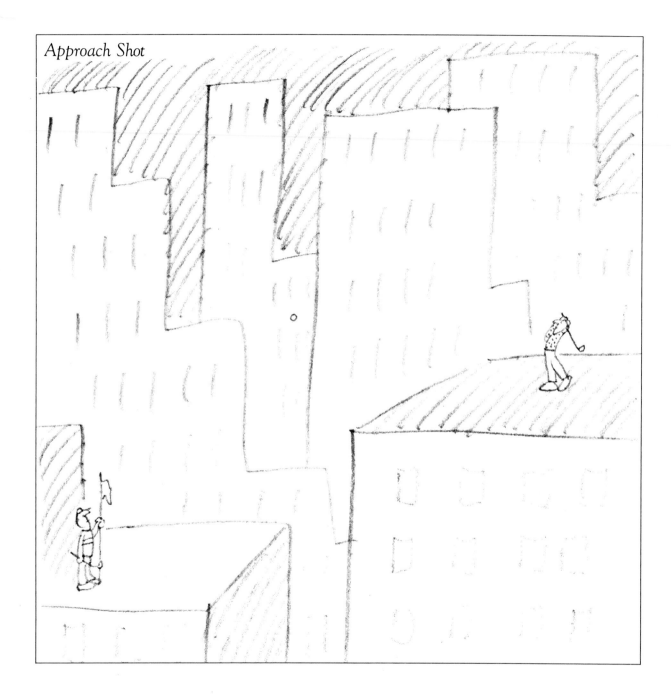

Amateur Golfer	One who plays golf for pleasure.
Analyst	Psychiatric specialist who treats individuals suffering from the delusion that playing golf is a form of pleasure.
Approach Shot	A shot which, if it had not caught the lip of the bunker and dropped back into the sand, would have rolled across the green and gone into the water. *See* CHIP SHOT and PITCH.
Apron	Fringe of low grass, or "frog hair," surrounding the green from which a tricky, easily muffed shot that is half pitch and half putt is made. It is called a "chupp," a "putch" or, simply, "chitt!"
Away	The player whose ball lies farthest from the hole is "away" and is required by the rules of golf to make the first shot. If, after the stroke is taken, the ball still lies farthest from the hole, the rules permit the player to kick the first bag and throw the first club.

B

Back Door	The side of the cup opposite the position of a player's ball on the green. Sometimes a putt will curve around the cup and enter by the "back door." Of course, on other occasions, it may choose to wait politely on the "back steps," sit down for a smoke on the "back porch" or go for a nice long walk in the "back yard."
Back Nine	The final 27 holes of an 18-hole golf course.
Backswing	The part of the swing that takes place after the ball has been improperly addressed but before it has been sent to the wrong destination. *See* FOLLOW-THROUGH.

Ball	A dimpled, rubber-covered, solid- or composite-cored, high-compression sphere with a weight of 1.62 ounces and a diameter of 1.68 inches that will enter a cup 4.25 inches in diameter and 4.0 inches deep after an average of 3.87 putts.
Ballwasher	Golfers who have "brushed up" on their tee tactics know that in addition to removing dirt from balls, the ubiquitous ballwasher also has a squeaky plunger that can be operated during an opponent's set-up to make certain that he or she is "in a lather" when the ball is hit, and they've learned that the pipe the machine is mounted on will produce a nerve-racking, swing-wrecking gong-like tone if struck with a clubhead, guaranteeing that their competitor's drive is a "washout" and that if any money is riding on the hole, they will "clean up."
Banana Ball	*1.* Long, looping slice. *2.* Formal dance at an exclusive club.
Bent	The species of grass most often found on greens.
Bermuda & Blue	The species of grass most often found on fairways.
Bindweed, Bog Grass, Bullrushes, Eel Grass, Quack Grass, Reeds, Scutch, Sedge, Spurge, Stinkweed & Viper's Grass	The species of grass among which the ball is most often found.
Birdie	A Mulligan, the best of one or more practice swings, and a 20-foot "gimme" putt. *See* EAGLE.

Ballwasher

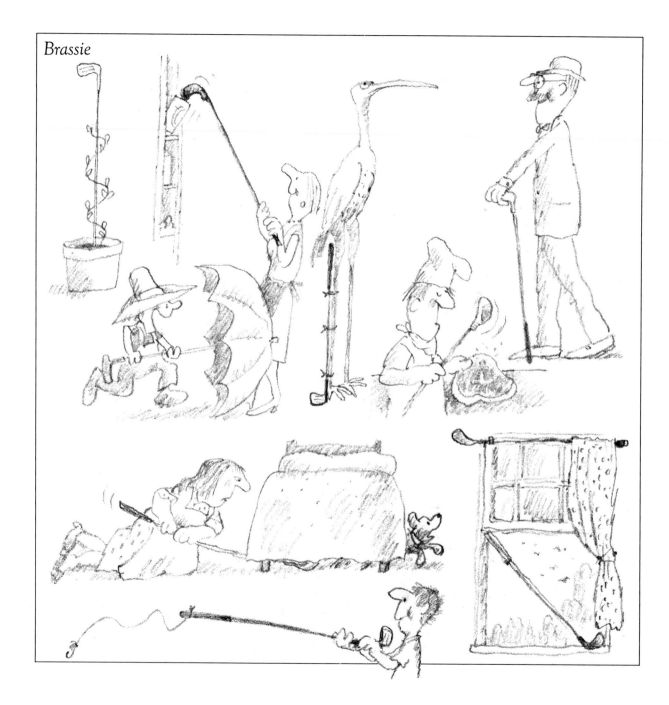

Brassie

Bisque	An informal handicapping system in which one player allows another to take a "free" stroke, called a "bisque," at whichever hole he or she chooses. Such a stroke taken without explicit permission from another player is a "tisque-tisque."
Blind Hole	A hole whose green is not visible when an approach shot is made, thereby requiring a player to rely on senses other than sight, such as the unmistakable sound of an unseen golfer shouting after being struck by a ball, the distinct smell of trouble, the metallic taste of fear and the sudden touch of flu that dictates an immediate return to the clubhouse by way of the deep woods.
Body English	Informal term for nervous leaning or twisting movements that players sometimes make, particularly while putting, to "persuade" the ball to go in a desired direction. If the ball fails to do so, these movements are often followed by a series of vulgar gestures and physical expressions of disgust referred to as body Spanish, body French or body Italian.
Bogey	The number of strokes needed to finish a hole by a golfer of average skill and above-average honesty. *See* DOUBLE BOGEY.
Brassie	Traditional name for the 2-wood, whose sole was at one time made of brass. The 3-wood is sometimes referred to as a "spoon," the 4-wood as a "baffie," the 5-iron as a "mashie," the 7-iron as a "mashie-niblick," and the 9-iron as a "niblick." Any club wrapped around a tree is a "smashie." If a club is flung into a water hazard, it is a "splashie." If it has a slippery grip, it is a "bashie." If it is hurled at a dog, it is a "lassie." A club that was allegedly used in a hole-in-one is a "fibstick." If it was a wood, it is a "fablespoon."

Caddy

Break	*1.* The shifting or changing of the direction of a putt caused by the slope or slant of a green. *2.* The splitting or shattering of the shaft of a putter caused by the rage or wrath of a player.
Bunker	A deep depression filled with sand filled with golfers in a deep depression.

C

Caddie	Individual who carries bags for golfers and assists them in the playing of the course. Ideally, a caddie should possess the eyes of a big-game hunter, the strength of a prop forward, the patience of a diplomat and the memory of a mafia witness.
Calamity Jane	Legendary golfer Bobby Jones' nickname for his "straight-shooting" putter. Few contemporary golfers give their putters nicknames, but those who do usually choose more appropriate sobriquets like "Runaround Sue" and "Unsinkable Molly Brown."
Carry	*1.* The distance travelled by a golf ball from the place where it is struck to the spot where it first touches the ground. *2.* The distance travelled by a golf ball in the pocket of a golfer from a place where it is unplayable to a spot where it may be surreptitiously dropped.
Casual Water	A temporary accumulation of water. The rules of golf provide that a ball may be moved without penalty from any non-permanent wet area, such as a rain puddle. Tears, however, no matter how copious, do not constitute casual water.

Chip Shot

Chip Shot	A short, low approach shot that gets a player into position for one or more missed putts. *See* PITCH.
Cleek	*1.* Old-fashioned chipping iron. *2.* Lateral water hazard on the legendary 8th hole ("The Poisoned Lotus") of the Royal Hong Kong golf course in Fanling.
Club Weight	There are three ways to measure the weight of a club: its overall weight, which ranges from about 13 ounces for a driver to just over 16 for a sand wedge; its swingweight, which is arrived at using a complex calculation of the relationship between the distribution of mass among a club's components and the length of its shaft; and its "bringweight," which is an estimate of its apparent heaviness on the 18th fairway on an afternoon in July and ranges between 21 and 46 pounds.
Clubface	The metal or wooden striking surface that is located on the front of a clubhead above the sole and between the toe and the heel. There is a specific point on every clubface called the "sweet spot," which, when it connects with a ball, produces maximum accuracy and power as well as a solid, gratifying feeling of perfect contact. It is difficult to say exactly where the sweet spot is since it varies from club to club, but generally speaking it is in the dead centre of the "bland belt," which is very near the "rotten region," in the middle of the "lousy area" and surrounded by the "loathsome zone."
Clubhead Covers	Wool or leather "mittens" slipped over the heads of woods to keep them dry. Zip-on coverings that encase the entire club in wetsuit material are also available and permit the eventual re-use of a favourite club flung into a water hazard, assuming that blind rage was tempered with foresight.

Clubhouse	Place where the rules are prominently posted.
Committee	The duly authorized drafters of the rules.
Competition	Form of play clearly established in the rules.
Course	Area of play strictly regulated under the rules.
Courtesy	Type of conduct specifically mandated by the rules.
Crap	The rules.
Cup	The metal or plastic cylinder fitted into the hole in the green. Strictly speaking, it is only the *lining* of the hole, but in regular golf usage players will often say "cup" when they mean "hole," just as they frequently will say "just in bounds" when they mean "out of bounds," "Oh, here it is" when they mean "I can't find it" and "five" when they mean "seven."

D

Delay	Golfers are expected to play "without undue delay." The question of exactly what constitutes undue delay has been under intensive study since 1971.
Dimples	Tiny circular hollows impressed onto the outer covering of golf balls to regulate their lift. The surface is also usually punctuated with at least one large cut, or "smile," caused by a shanked iron shot. Curiously, golfers who complete these "faces" by adding eyes, ears, hair and a nose to roughly resemble whoever taught them golf find that they can hit their works of art nearly twice the distance of an undecorated ball.

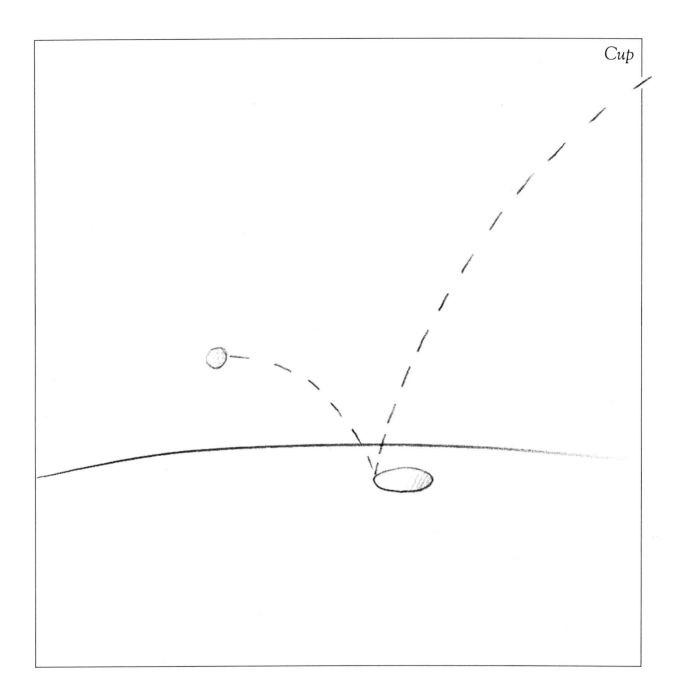

Cup

Divot

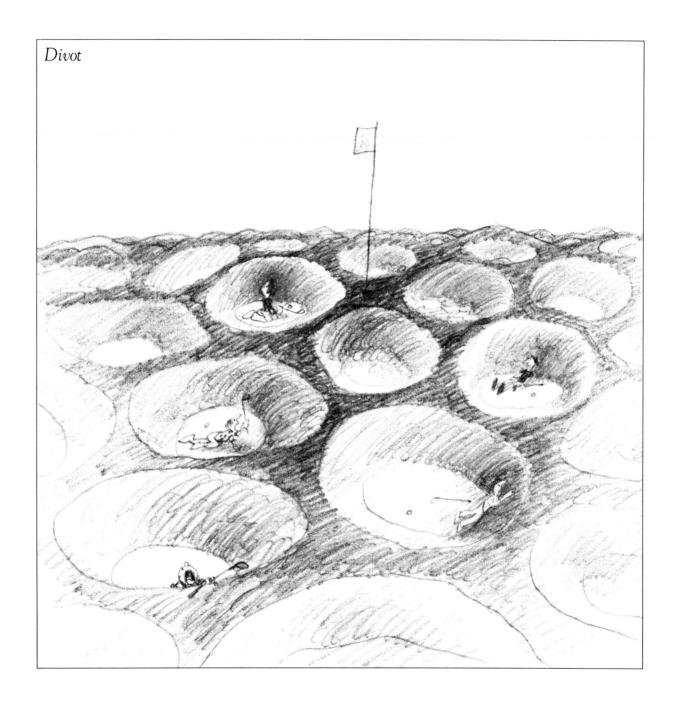

Divot	Colourful Scottish word for the piece of turf scooped from the ground in front of the ball in the course of an iron shot. In Scotland, depending on its size, a divot is referred to as a "wee tuftie" (2″ x 4″), "peg o' sward" (4″ x 6″), "snatch of haugh" (6″ x 8″), "fine tussock" (8″ x 10″), "glen" (1′ x 2′), "firth" (1½′ x 3′), "loch" (2′ x 4′) and "damned English divot" (anything larger than 8 square feet).
Dogleg	A hole with a 90° angle between the tee and the green. One with a pockmarked tee area, unkempt fairways or a patchy green is a "dogear." One on which large amounts of casual water regularly accumulate is a "dog paddle." One with an elevated tee and green and a sunken, treacherous approach is a "dog dish." And a course on which holes like these predominate is, simply, a "dog."
Dormie	Formal term for a team in match play that leads by as many holes as remain to be played. "Hustlers" will often deliberately shoot poorly during the early part of a round to get gullible opponents into this apparently favourable position, then propose a greatly increased, all-or-nothing bet on the remaining holes, with a sudden-death playoff if necessary. How can you spot these tricksters? It's not easy, but, generally speaking, don't play golf for money with players who use two-piece clubs that unscrew in the center of the shaft, who put baby powder on their hands before grasping the driver or use billiard chalk on their clubfaces, or who have a habit of saying things like "Dunlop 4 in the center pocket" before making a putt.
Double Bogey	Two strokes over par, or, for a golfer who happened to score a 7 on a long par-5, a birdie and an eagle that occurred on the same hole. *See* TRIPLE BOGEY.

Double Eagle

Three strokes less than par for a given hole. This unusual achievement might be accomplished by, say, taking advantage of a tailwind on a straight par-5 hole to get down in two strokes, scoring a hole-in-one on a short par-4 or just skipping entirely a difficult par-3 hole. *See* HOLE-IN-ONE.

Dress

Although clothes in a variety of styles are acceptable on a golf course, a few general pointers are worth keeping in mind when selecting an outfit:

○ It should be visible to an individual with normal eyesight looking out the window of a spacecraft in orbit.
○ It should be made out of a fabric derived from a substance that was mined or refined rather than grown or raised.
○ It should jam radar.
○ It should be composed of no fewer than eight separate colours or shades and should bear a minimum of four distinct emblems.
○ When scuffed, the shoes should require repainting or replastering rather than shining.
○ Any hat should be identifiable as such only by its position on the wearer's head.

Drive

The initial shot on each hole, made with a special wood, the driver, on par-4 and par-5 holes, and with shorter woods or irons on par-3 holes. Because the drive is so critical to the play of the hole, total concentration is essential, and thus, if the shot is spoiled because of some audible disturbance inadvertently caused by another player on the tee, such as a pair of shoelace tips clicking together or the wind whistling through an onlooker's eyelashes, it is customary to take the shot again. *See* MULLIGAN.

PRO · AMATEUR

Driving Iron	The number 1 iron, sometimes used for tee shots. Its chief virtue is that, unlike a wooden-headed driver, it puts a deep cut in the ball while driving it into the rough or out of bounds, thus ensuring that if the golfer who hit the ball cannot find it, no other player will get any use out of it.
Driving Range	A place where golfers go to get all the good shots out of their systems.
Dropping a Ball	A recent rule change does away with the old requirement that players introducing a ball to replace one that is lost do so by dropping it over their shoulder and behind their back. Players may now drop it at arm's length in any direction they choose. Of course, as before, a penalty stroke is assessed. This rule change does not affect clandestine ball drops, which are still made from the bottom edge of the trouser pocket with the thumb and first two fingers of one hand while idly swinging a club with the other. And, it goes without saying, there is still no penalty for such drops.
Duffer	A golfer whose actual score on any given hole is ordinarily more than twice his or her reported score.

E

Eagle	Unusually low score on a hole achieved by a golfer with an exceptionally good drive and one or two exceptionally good follow-up shots, or by a golfer with an exceptionally poor memory. *See* HOLE-IN-ONE.
Equipment	According to the rules of golf, equipment is "anything that can be thrown, broken, kicked, twisted, torn, crushed, shredded or mangled; or propelled, driven or directed,

Etiquette (Never Break a Player's Concentration)

either under its own power or by means of a transfer of momentum, into undergrowth, trees or other overgrown terrain; or over the edge of a natural or artificially elevated area; or below the surface of any body of water, whether moving or impounded."

Etiquette | The rules of behaviour in golf. There isn't room here for a complete list, but a few of the more important ones are:
- Never put tees in your nose.
- Never sneeze into your glove.
- Never concede a chip shot.
- Never hold a ball for another player to hit.
- Never practice drives against a backboard.
- Never wear golf shoes to a dance.

Explosion Shot | A shot in which, after a poorly swung sand wedge fails to contact enough sand, the ball flies off the face of the club and the player flies off the handle.

F

Fade | *1. (Right-handed golfers)* A shot that curves from left to right.
2. (Left-handed golfers) A shot that curves from right to left.

Fairway | A narrow strip of mown grass that separates two groups of golfers looking for lost balls in the rough.

Fairway Wood | A club with a medium loft that is used to get a ball out of a good lie on the fairway and into position for a shot from a slope, a bunker, a water hazard or behind a tree.

5th & 15th Holes | *See* RAIN.

Finesse Shot	Any non-standard shot used to get a ball out of an awkward or impossible lie by bending, twisting or stretching the rules or by hitting it directly through a loophole.
First Tee	*See* FLUFF, HOOK, SCLAFF, SHANK, SLICE, TOP and WHIFF.
Flagstick	Long, flexible metal pole with red-and-white markings along its length and a numbered flag at its top, which, had it not been left lying on the green by the previous foursome, would have indicated the position of the hole.
Flub	A shot that is too weak to register on conventional score-keeping equipment.
Fluff	A shot in which the clubhead strikes the ground behind the ball before hitting it, causing it to dribble forward one or two yards. A more widely used term for this type of stroke is "practice swing." *See* WHIFF.
Follow-through	The part of the swing that takes place after the ball has been hit but before the club has been thrown. *See* SWING.
Fore	The first of several four-letter words exchanged between golfers as one group of players hits balls toward another in front of them on the course.
Four-ball	A match in which two pairs of players each play their better ball against the other. Additional golf matches include: best-ball, in which one player plays against the better ball of two or the best ball of three players; three-ball, in which three players play against one another, each playing his or her own ball; and no-ball, in which two, three or four players, all of whom have lost all their balls, go to the clubhouse and play gin rummy.

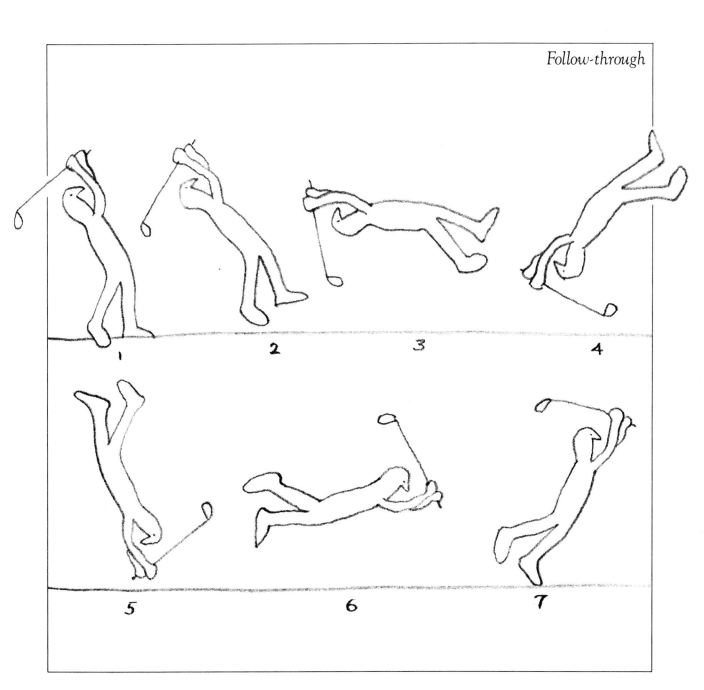

1

2

3

4

5

6

7

Foursome

Four-putt	To take four strokes of the putter to put the ball into the hole after driving it onto the green. *See* ONE-PUTT.
Foursome	Four golfers playing a round together. Four golfers who tee off before the group ahead of them is entirely clear is a 'fearsome'. A foursome of golfers who insist on giving advice while other players make their drives is a 'meddlesome'. Four ladies playing erratically is a 'troublesome'. A group of players involved in a protracted discussion of their scores is a 'quarrelsome'. Four golfers who all know the Rules of Golf by heart is a 'tiresome'. And any foursome of players who are not themselves delayed and yet still require more than 4 hours to complete 18 holes is a 'loathsome'.
Front Nine	The first half of an 18-hole golf course. A golfer who, by the end of the 9th hole, has shot within a few strokes of par for 18 is entitled to skip the second half of the course and head directly for the 19th hole.

G

Gallery	The spectators at a golf tournament. Golf fans enjoy a much higher degree of participation in their favourite sport than their counterparts seated in stadiums could ever dream of: they get almost as much exercise as the players themselves, they can wear the identical playing outfits without the slightest embarrassment, they stand at least as good a chance of being injured during the course of play as even the top golfer in the country does, and they can enter upon and do serious damage to the playing field before and during the contest as well as after it is over.

Game	A competitive round of golf, but also a particular golfer's style of play. Over time, golfers tend to progress through several basic kinds of "game": great drives, poor approach shots and lousy putting; awful drives, foul approach shots and superb putting; perfect drives, rotten approach shots and dreadful putting; and ping-pong, bowls and croquet.
Gimme	A conceded putt, usually one measured in inches; e.g., a 2-inch putt, a 5-inch putt, an 11-inch putt, a 94-inch putt or a 2,844-inch putt. *See* IN THE LEATHER.
Golf	The derivation of the word "golf" from its Celtic and Middle English roots is obscure. Some possibilities are: *gilff* (an incurable madness), *gylf* (a notorious liar), *gullf* (to beat a shrub with a short stick), *golve* (under; beneath; lost; blocked; submerged; stuck; obstructed), *gellvo* (horribly; terribly; hopelessly; awfully), *galfa* (my God!; oh, no!), *goulfyl* (to cry; to weep) and *gaelf* (I quit). *See* KOLVEN.
Golf Accessories	Gadgets whose purchase improves players' games primarily by eliminating bulk from their wallets, thereby reducing excessive trouser friction and allowing a smooth hip movement in the swing.
Golf Bag	Portable container with compartments designed to hold clubs, balls and other golfing accessories. There are two basic types of golf bag, and serious players usually own one of each: an inexpensive canvas or nylon "carry" bag that would have been easy to lug around the home course if the shoulder strap hadn't broken on the 3rd tee, and a more durable vinyl or leather "travel" bag that would have been used on a golf trip if the airline had not sent it to a continent other than the one on which the course its owner planned to play is located.

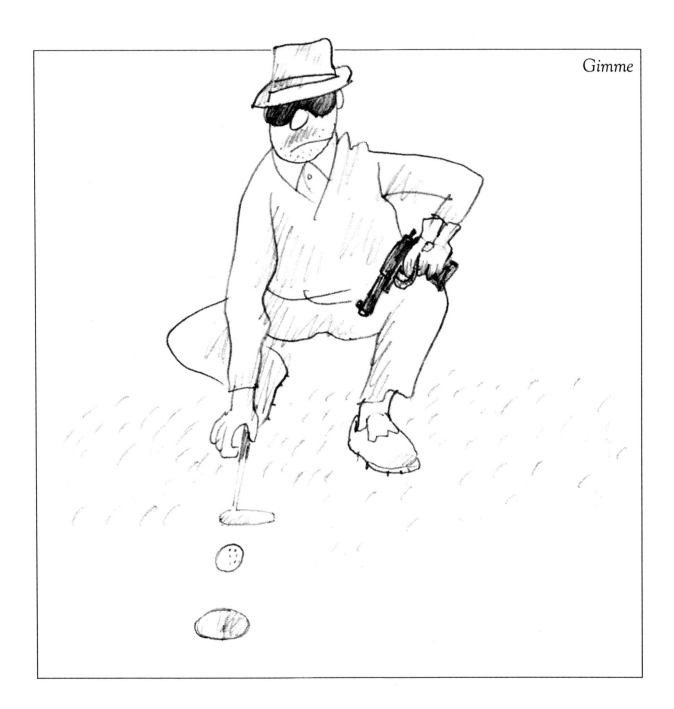

Golf Cart

Two-wheeled bag carrier that decreases the exercise value of playing 18 holes of golf from about the level of two sets of doubles tennis to the equivalent of an hour and a half of shopping. With a four-wheeled electric cart, the physical demands of the game can be reduced even further to about the same as 10 minutes of rearranging sofa cushions, watering a dozen plants or one complete loading and unloading of a dishwasher.

Golf Club

1. The basic implement in golf, which consists of a long shaft on one end of which is the head, which is attached to the shaft at the heel and has on one side a distinct face. 2. A social organization built around a golf course and composed of a number of heels, a membership committee head with two faces, and a long waiting list of people who are going to get the shaft.

Golf Glove

An unpleasant odour worn on the hand.

Golf Grippe

Mysterious ailment whose sudden but short-lived symptoms of violent coughing and sneezing usually occur on the tee or green. It can often be cured by pounding the sufferer vigorously on the back with a 5-iron.

Golf Shoes

There are two basic kinds of special footwear that golfers can choose from: traditional golf shoes with metal spikes and the newer rubber-studded models. There are a number of differences between the two designs, but the question of which type to select really boils down to whether you want a shoe that you can blame for spoiling your shot because its spikes caught in the turf during your backswing or one you can blame because its studs slipped in the grass during your downswing.

Golf Cart

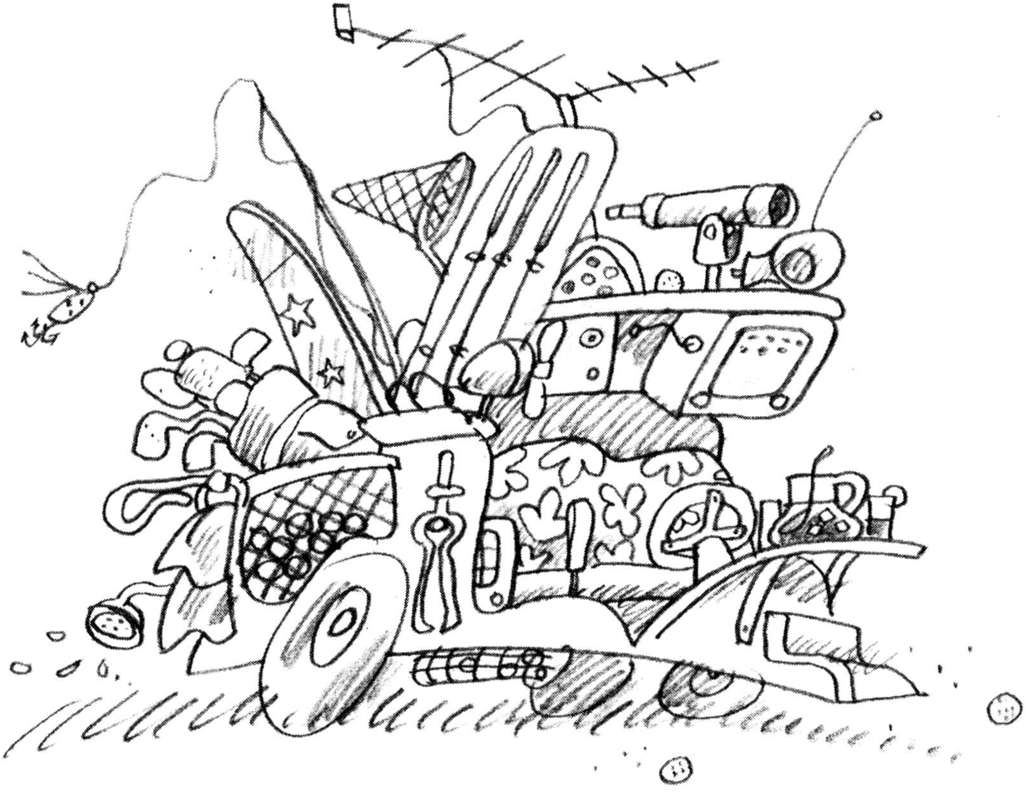

Golf Widow

Non-playing wife of an obsessive golfer. Just for the record, judges have consistently decided that although golf clearly is "extreme mental cruelty," it is not grounds for divorce since "the unspeakable sufferings are experienced exclusively by the player and not by the one abandoned as the result of such play" (*Humphrey v. Humphrey*). On the other hand, courts have been equally firm in throwing out wills altered in favour of favourite golf holes (*Alexander v. Trust for the Mowing of the Rough on the Back Nine at Royal Toppingham C.C.*), bequests to dubious sporting foundations (*Bennett v. The Society for the Perfection of the Backswing*) and posthumous gifts for the care and preservation of treasured clubs (*Howard v. Irons, Woods, et al.*).

Golfing

A pastime that gives people cooped up in the office all week a chance to lie and cheat outdoors.

Golfing Holiday

Period of time spent playing golf in a place where the rain is warm or where notices indicating that a course is closed due to inclement weather are posted in a foreign language.

Green

A roughly circular area of smooth, lush grass whose verdant hue is the result of regular sprinkling and constant sobbing, bawling, blubbering and whimpering.

Greenie & Sandy

Two popular side bets in which the players in a foursome agree to ante up a small amount of money to be awarded to the first player on the green on each hole ("greenie") and to any of their number who get out of a sand trap and into the hole in two strokes ("sandy"). Other common golfing wagers include paying a set sum of money to the player who uttered the fewest four-letter words during the round ("cleanie") and the player who threw the smallest number of clubs ("Gandhi").

Hazard

Green Fee
The charge for playing a round of golf. When paying this fee, mediocre players should keep in mind the fact that whereas golfers who regularly shoot par are shelling out nearly fifty pence for every shot they take, a hopeless duffer is paying a mere ten or fifteen p. a stroke.

Grip
The end of the club that slips, twists, rips or flakes, as distinct from the end of the club that rusts, splits, chips or cracks. *See* HEAD.

H

Half
In match play, to tie a hole. Thus, if player A and player B both have a 5 on the 14th hole, they have "halved" the hole. Incidentally, that phrase is pronounced "they have haved" because the "l" in "halve" is silent, a fascinating fact that player A may want to discuss with player B during the latter's backswing on the 15th tee.

Handicap
An allocation of strokes on one or more holes that permits two golfers of very different ability to do equally poorly on the same course.

Hazard
A man-made obstacle on the course, either a bunker or a water hazard. It is against the rules for players to "ground" their clubs in a hazard, i.e., to allow the clubhead to touch the sand or water before making their shots. They may, however, bury their own head in their hands, strike their forehead with the base of their palms, shake their head vigorously from side to side (with or without their hand placed on their brow) and, if it does not delay the match, lightly and repeatedly tap their head against a tree.

Head	The end of the club that produces cock-ups and mis-hits as opposed to the end of the club that produces calluses and blisters. *See* GRIP.
Hickory	Tough, resilient wood originally used for golf club shafts. The chromed steel tubing employed today has superior strength and durability, but old-time golfers insist that there is nothing more satisfying than the crisp snap of a hickory-shafted club being broken sharply across the knee or the delicate aroma of an entire set of clubs burning merrily in a fireplace.
Hole	*1.* To hit the ball into the hole, as in "I *holed* my putt for a five." *2.* The cup in the green into which the ball is hit, as in "Five? Try again, friend—you're in the *hole* in twelve." *3.* One of 9 or 18 playing areas constituting a golf course, as in "On that *hole* I had a drive, two approach shots and two putts—that makes five." *4.* A missing element or discrepancy in a narrative or a fault or flaw in logic or reasoning, as in "Your story is full of *holes*—what about those two lost balls, the stroke in the water hazard and the out-of-bounds shot?" *5.* An aperture or opening, as in "You have a *hole* in your head—those were practice swings." *6.* Indebtedness, as in "You lost, you weasel—you're in the *hole* to me for fifty quid." *7.* An embarrassing predicament or position, as in "Oh, yeah? Well, I'm not paying, so how do you like that? But you fork out fifty smackers or you'll be in a real *hole* at work when I tell your boss about how when you're supposed to be with your clients you're out on the golf course and your wife about that blonde you met on the putting green and—" *8.* An excavation or cavity, as in "The body was found in a shallow *hole* in a sand trap by the thirteenth green."

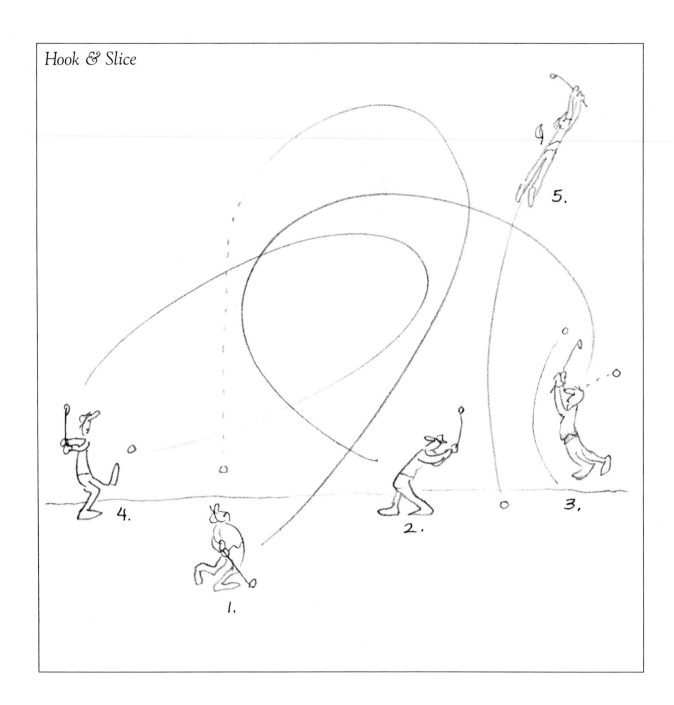

Hook & Slice

Hole-in-One

An occurrence in which a ball is hit directly from the tee into the hole on a single shot by a golfer playing alone.

Home Course

A place where your chief handicap is that everyone knows exactly what it is.

Honour

The privilege of being laughed at first on the tee.

Hook & Slice

To hit a shot that curves sharply left (hook) or right (slice), respectively. Players who do one or the other should consider changing the way they stand, hold the club, or swing. Players who do both should consider changing the way they spend their weekends.

I

Identifying the Ball

Except in a hazard, players may, without incurring a penalty, lift a ball they think is theirs and clean it for purposes of identification. After doing so, they must put it back in exactly the same spot from which they took it. However, most golfers are aware that in the few seconds needed to complete this manoeuvre, the earth itself has moved in a number of directions, both because of its own rotation and due to the movements it shares with the solar system and the galaxy, and they compensate for these motions by shifting the position of the ball from, say, the muddy divot hole from which it was removed to a point a few trillionths of an Astronomical Unit away (about a foot) occupied by a nice tuft of grass.

Impossible Lie

A ball that is in a position that is both completely obstructed by an immovable object and continuously observed by an incorruptible player.

Instruction

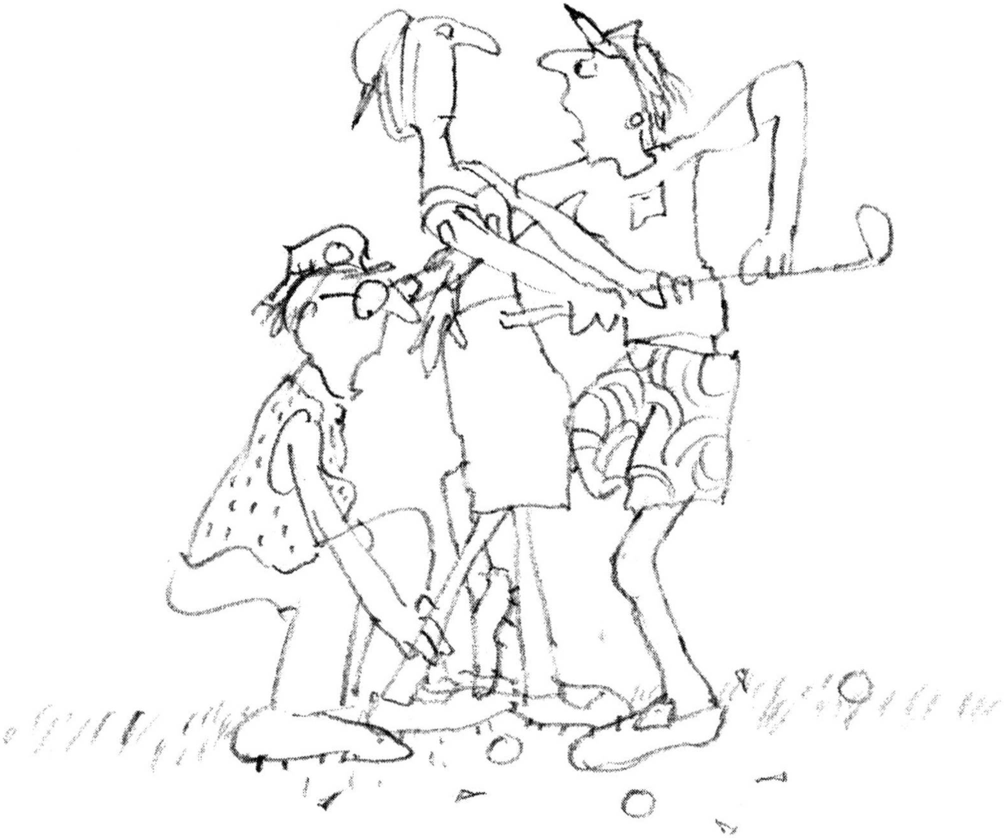

In the Leather

A phrase which indicates that a putt is close enough to the hole to be conceded. A putter is placed on the green with its head in the cup to determine whether or not the putt in question is even with or below the beginning of the grip, and if it is, it's a gimme. Many players find this procedure unnecessarily restrictive and generally agree on a policy of making concessions if a putt is "in the local dialing area." *See* GIMME.

Instruction

Golf is virtually impossible to learn from a book, and some personalized instruction is absolutely essential, but there are a handful of simple admonitions that every player would do well to commit to memory:
o Don't lock your knees.
o Don't bend your left arm.
o Don't loosen your grip.
o Don't pick up your head.
o Don't count out loud.
o Don't write in ink on your scorecard.

Irons

1. Penology. Variously shaped pieces of metal by the use of which individuals are subjected to torment. *2. Golf.* Variously shaped pieces of metal by the use of which individuals are subjected to torment.

J

Jigger

1. Traditional short pitching iron used to get out of trouble on holes 1 through 18. *2.* Traditional short measuring glass used to get into trouble at hole 19.

Junior

A golfer who attributes poor play to the fact that he or she lacks the experience of a mature player. *See* SENIOR.

K

Keeping Score

In general, golfers assign a number exactly one higher than the previous one for each shot they play to arrive at the cumulative total of all the strokes required to complete a given hole. While it has the merit of simplicity, this system does tend to produce discouragingly high numbers, and players who perennially score in the 90s or higher might think about switching to an unconventional numbering system which, while still adhering strictly to the custom of counting each and every stroke, nevertheless provides a more acceptable result. Two excellent candidates are the arithmetic series -2,-1,0,1,2,3,4 etc. and 1,2,2,3,3,3,4,4,4,4 etc. Also worth considering are binary numbers, which, no matter how large, are always composed of zeros and ones, and Roman numerals, whose simple written form (the key golf numbers 4,5,6,7 and 8 are indicated by IV,V,VI,VII and VIII) permits alteration of the scorecard with the effortless erasure or addition of an "I" or two rather than the complex conversion of, say, a telltale Arabic "9" into a "5."

Knickerbockers

Baggy trousers worn by golfers in the 1930s. They were called "plus fours" because they were cut off four inches below the knee, then tucked into long socks. Plus fours have almost disappeared from golf courses, and the only golfing apparel anything like them that exists today is a much more appealing form of attire, worn by women, known as "minus tens."

Kolven

A golf-like 17th-century Dutch game played on frozen canals with clubs and balls. A similar game called "chole" was being played in France in the 14th century, and there are other, even earlier traces of the sport. For example, in the modest tomb of King Puttankhamen I (1350 B.C.?-1345 B.C.?), a set of 14 bronze-shafted clubs were discovered, each one broken in two; and, in eastern Turkey, an ancient Babylonian clay tablet from about 4000 B.C. was unearthed that bears an astonishing resemblance to a scorecard, with the numbers 1 to 18 inscribed in a row and, next to them, scores (a few of them changed several times) that add up to 117 but are followed in the space for a total at the bottom of the column by the number 77.

L

Ladies' Days & Hours

Times set aside by a golf club during which the use of the course is exclusively reserved for women players, who are sometimes barred at other times. The number of women playing golf has increased dramatically in recent years, but as the institution of Ladies' Days and Hours indicates, their presence on courses is still objectionable to male players who take the game of golf very seriously and resent the sudden intrusion into their hallowed pastime of the lady golfer, whose insistence on actually hitting balls toward the holes interferes with the conduct of business deals, interrupts the recounting of lengthy comic narratives, and impedes the timely exchange of critical information on the recent performance of cars and the relative prospects of sports teams.

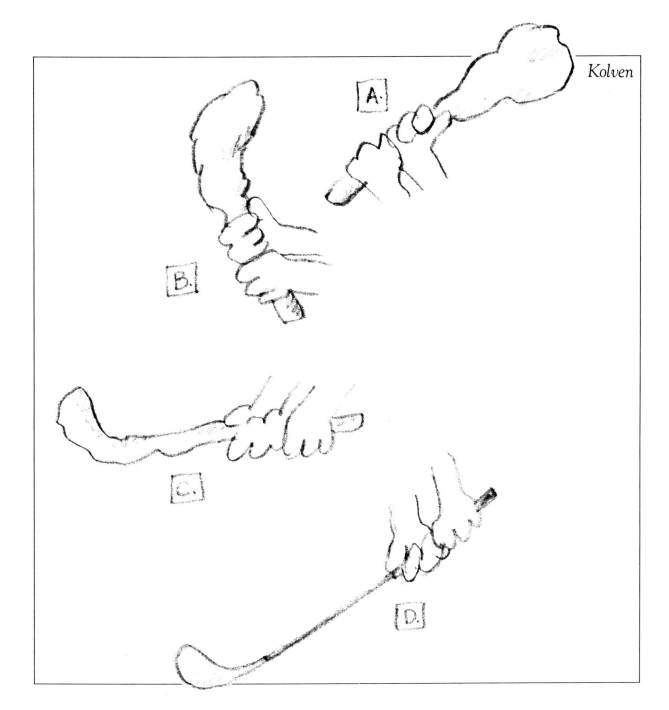

Kolven

A.

B.

C.

D.

Lie (1.)

Ladies' Tees	Teeing areas placed somewhat closer to the greens to compensate for the fact that although women are as capable as men of playing first-rate golf, they do not, as a rule, hit the ball as far. Other allowances made for women golfers to permit them to hold their own during rounds with male players include giving them, along with their scorecards, a copy of the *Financial Times*, a booklet of old jokes and a laminated card on which is printed key data on the recent performance of various cars and cricket teams.
Lag	A long putt played conservatively to make sure that the ball ends up near enough to the hole to be sunk with the next stroke. If this putt is missed, it is referred to as an "aaag."
Left-handed Golfers	Although golf, with its overwhelming right-handed orientation, penalizes left-handed players more than other sports do, it also provides two significant advantages to "south-grips": most golfers can't borrow your spare golf glove and they can't demonstrate the "right way to swing that club" after you muff your drive.
Legs	A ball is said to have "legs" if it continues to roll a significant distance after landing. If it bounces into the rough and becomes wedged under a rock or in the crook of a tree, it is said to have "claws." If it runs down a bank and into a water hazard, it has "fins." If, on a putt, it rings the cup without going in, it has "lips." And if it does all these things on the same hole, it is given "wings" and flung into the bushes.
Lie	*1.* Where the ball comes to rest after being hit by a golfer. *2.* The number of strokes it took to get it there, as reported by that golfer.

Links	Golf courses are often referred to as "links," but, strictly speaking, this term applies only to a course laid out over the natural contours of the bleak, wind-swept land along the sea, as was the original course at St. Andrews. At first glance, the lush golf courses in the U.S. seem to bear little resemblance to their austere Scottish progenitor, but tradition is very important in the game of golf and American clubs have made every effort to be true to their Highland roots. For example, no towel in any golf club's locker room exceeds 2 square feet in area or $1/20$th of an inch in thickness; no light bulb in any washroom is ever of a wattage greater than 25; no radiator in any dressing room achieves a temperature higher than 66°, nor is hot water ever warmer than 88°; walls are painted only in years divisible by 16, and no object or mechanism is replaced until the end of the decade in which it first broke or ceased to function; and all facilities for women are faithfully patterned after the original Wee Lassies' Changing Boothy in a leaky greenskeeper's hut overlooking the Firth of Fife.
Lip	*1.* Perimeter of grass surrounding the hole. *2.* Remarks made by fellow golfer when your putt stops there.
Local Rules	A set of regulations that are ignored only by players on one specific course rather than by golfers as a whole.
Loft	The angle of a clubface and the corresponding steepness of the shot it will produce. Loft angles range from the relatively shallow ones used for long, unobstructed shots (12° for a driver, 20° for a fairway wood, 30° for a 5-iron) to the much steeper ones needed to clear obstacles (47° for a 9-iron, 58° for a sand wedge, 75° for the tip of a golf shoe, and up to 100° for a throwing arm).

Lost Ball

Loose Impediments	Natural and legally movable objects that interfere with play, such as dazed or disoriented reptiles or mammals, stunned birds, pulverized stones, flattened bushes, uprooted shrubs, severed branches and felled trees. *See* OBSTRUCTIONS.
Lost Ball	An opponent's missing ball after 90 seconds of searching, or one of your own after 20 minutes.
Low Side	The side of a hole on a sloping green that gravity tends to send a ball away from. Canny golfers always aim for the "high side" of the hole or lay the flagstick along the edge of the cup and putt toward this "safe side."

M

Mark	Any small object, such as a coin or tee, placed directly behind a ball to indicate a point on the green that is 5 inches farther from the hole than the spot where the ball will be replaced.
Match Play	Golfing competition whose outcome is determined by calculating which team or individual had the lowest score on the most holes.
Medal Play	Golfing competition whose outcome is determined by calculating which player had the lowest overall score for 18 holes.
Melee Play	Golfing competition whose outcome is determined by a fistfight on the 18th green.
Mixed Foursome	A quartet of golfers composed of two separate grounds for divorce.

19th Hole

Mulligan	A second, provisional ball played following a tee shot that may be lost or unplayable. If the first ball is indeed lost or unplayable, the "Mulligan" is then played with a one-stroke penalty. If the provisional ball is played, but the player forgets or declines to add the penalty stroke to his or her score, it's a "Haldeman." If the player finds the original ball in a playable but inconvenient position, surreptitiously pockets it and plays the provisional ball, again without penalty, it's an "Ehrlichman." If a player steals a ball from an opponent's bag to play as a provisional ball, then counts neither the stroke used to hit it nor a penalty stroke, it's a "Nixon."

N

Nassau	A golf scoring system that allocates one point to the winner of each 9 holes and one to the winner of the 18. This system is a favourite among high-stakes players. Of course, no one on a golf course with even the remotest idea of what constitutes proper behaviour in the game of golf would dream of placing a wager on the outcome of a round. However, since there is no one on any golf course who has even the remotest idea of what constitutes proper behaviour in the game of golf, betting is universal.
19th Hole	The only hole on which golfers do not complain about the number of shots they took.
Numbers	A player's score after the subtraction of his or her handicap from the Gross Score is the Net Score. Adding strokes for each Mulligan yields the True Score. If whiffs and fluffs are also counted, the resulting tabulation is the Real Score. If strokes for lost balls, improved lies, and shots hit

out of bounds are included as well, the grand total is the Actual Score. This number, when adjusted upward to reflect all gimme putts, becomes the Correct Score. When all the strokes made in sand traps and around obstructions are tacked on, this larger sum is the Absolute, Final, Honest-to-Goodness Score, which is usually only a half-dozen or so strokes lower than the total number of shots the player in fact made.

Obstructions

Golfers may move their balls away from or remove any artificial obstacles not part of the course such as torn and crushed hats and other discarded articles of clothing; chewed scorecards; ripped instruction books; halved golf balls; discarded golf clubs; demolished handcarts; and overturned and burning electric carts.

Official Records

The history of golf is filled with the memorable accomplishments of the game's stars, but, alas, the more humble achievements of less skilled players often go unsung. The brief list below is an attempt to rectify this unfortunate state of affairs:

SHORTEST MISSED PUTT: .83 inch, Angus McNaith, 9th Green, Loch Dorrach.

LONGEST SUSTAINED SCREAM: 39 seconds, Elizabeth Swansdowne, 8th tee, Duffingdale.

SHARPEST BEND IN ONE MOTION: 314°, Miguel Vallejo, 15th hole, Torquemada.

FARTHEST THROWN CLUB: 86.4 yards, Pierre LaFontaine, 4th hole, Saint-Auban-sur-Baguette.

One-putt	To send the ball into the hole with one stroke of a putter after taking 11 shots to reach the green. *See* FOUR-PUTT.
Open	A tournament that is open to all players, amateur or professional, who can qualify. Big tournaments like the British and U.S. Opens are the goal of any talented golfer, but it is worth remembering that whereas in, say, tennis only 50 percent of the players in the men's singles final will lose, in golf more than 98 percent of the players in the final round of a tournament invariably fail to win.
Out of Bounds	A ball lies out of bounds and may not be played if the whole of its circumference is beyond the line marked by the stakes that form the golf course boundary. Many golfers feel, however, that a ball which appears to be out of bounds should, considering the curvature of the earth, be more properly regarded as in bounds since it lies a good 24,900 miles inside the out-of-bounds line.
Overclubbing & Underclubbing	Using clubs that hit the ball over your target ("too much club") or short of it ("too little club") is a common mistake made by many players. You can overcome this error by understanding what each club can do, and meanwhile you can compensate by overlooking and undercounting, and, if caddies are present, by overtipping with an understanding.

P

Par	Score achieved by a golfer who had only a few great shots on an entire round but somehow managed to hit them all on the same hole. *See* TRIPLE BOGEY.

Partner

Partner	Match play team member who holes out from a bunker to score a birdie on a hole you were about to win with a tap-in for a par, then putts out for a double bogey on a hole where you lie six and your ball is 40 feet from the cup.
Penalty	One or more strokes added to a golfer's score for play in contravention of the rules. Players are penalized a single stroke for simple infractions, such as Lost Ball, Ball Out of Bounds and Unplayable Ball. More serious breaches, like Playing Wrong Ball and Stopping or Deflecting Own Ball, carry a penalty of two strokes. The most severe violations, for which penalties ranging from three to five strokes are assessed, include: Pocketing Opponent's Lost Ball, Kicking Opponent's Ball Out of Bounds, Feeding Opponent's Ball to a Dog, and Rendering Opponent's Ball Unplayable by Running Over It with an Electric Golf Cart.
Pin	Familiar term for the flagstick. A ball that lands on the green even with the hole but off to one side is "pin high." A ball that lands right next to the hole, leaving a very short putt, is "stiff to the pin." Such putts are almost always conceded, but some players insist on putting them anyway. These players are called "pinheads."
Pin Placement	The location of the hole in each green is changed regularly to distribute wear evenly over the grass surface and to create an additional challenge to golfers familiar with the course. And, as golfers whose balls mysteriously land in a pond or bunker they've successfully avoided for months can attest, the position of key sand traps and water hazards is also periodically shifted and the astronomical cost of operating heavy earthmoving equipment at night and in secret explains the high greens fees charged at most golf courses.

Pitch

An approach shot made with a short iron. There are four basic kinds of pitch shot: one in which the ball is given top spin to let it run along the green towards the cup (pitch-and-run); one in which it is given backspin to make it "sit down" and stop next to the cup (pitch-and-stop); one in which it is shanked into a water hazard or dense undergrowth (pitch-and-search or pitch-and-destroy); and one in which it is driven directly into the ground with a half-top (pitch-and-moan).

Play It as It Lies

One of the two fundamental dictates of golf. The other one is "Wear It if It Clashes."

Playing Through

A display of courtesy on the course in which a group of golfers who have stopped to search for lost balls conclude that they are causing delay and, anxious to spare the group behind them several minutes of inactivity on the tee, stand aside and invite that group to hit their drives so they will be able to profitably use the period before they can resume play in a time-consuming hunt for their own lost balls.

Practice Green

A putting area near the clubhouse where players can try out chips, pitches and putts. It is usually located near the 19th hole so players can also work on their nips, draughts and snorts.

Practice Tee

The place where golfers go to convert a nasty hook into a wicked slice.

Priority on the Course

In determining the order of play, the following rules should be applied:
○ Matches which, when Mulligans and practice shots are included, are playing 10, 12 or 14 balls should give way to matches playing 6 or 8 balls.

○ A match that is playing the course out of sequence by cutting across from the green of one hole to the tee of a much later hole is entitled to pass a match that sneaked onto the course without paying.

○ Any match that has a player in it posing as a doctor who is late for a vital operation takes precedence over a match with a player pretending to be a judge overdue at a key trial.

○ Single players have no standing and must give way to a match consisting of two, three or four golfers unless, through voice changes and variations in stance and gesture, they can convincingly fake the symptoms of a multiple personality disorder.

Pro

Sensible person who believes that individuals who spend time playing golf professionally are no different from those who engage in some other similarly demanding occupation such as strip mining or demolition work and that, far from paying for the privilege, they should actually receive financial compensation for their labours.

Pro Shop

Challenging hazard located just before the first tee at most clubs. The trick to getting out in under £10 (about par for the course) is concentration. Don't be distracted by the leather golf bags and matched club sets, the radical new putter designs, the smooth gloves, the shiny shoes, and the sporty golfing attire. Keep your head down and your eyes on the balls and tees. Tell yourself that your present clubs aren't old—they're classics. Every item of apparel you're wearing brings you luck. Your shoes are perfectly broken in. Your hat has character. Your glove . . . Forget your glove. Take a firm stance and dig in your heels. Get a good grip on your wallet. Take it out in a fast, sweeping motion and lightly flip a few crisp notes onto the counter. Always use cash: "charging" is one of the hardest golf habits to break, and those few little pen strokes can end up costing you plenty. Pick up your purchase with a quick snap of the wrist, then turn and stride confidently for the tee. You may shoot 100 today, but you're way, way ahead of the game!

Pull	To hit a shot straight but to the left of the intended target.
Push	To hit a shot straight but to the right of the intended target.
Putt	To hit a shot straight but to the left, the right, beyond, short of, over or around the intended target.
Putter	Specialized club used on the green. The putter differs from the other golf clubs in the bag in that it *always* produces shots that roll forward a few feet and stop.

Q

Quoits	Along with curling and tossing the caber, the only game other than golf that has been voted Most Pointless Athletic Pursuit of the Decade more than three times by the editors of *Stupid Sports Magazine*.

R

R&A	The Royal and Ancient Golf Club of St. Andrews, founded in 1754 and the oldest golf club in existence. As such, it holds many "firsts" in the game of golf: first accusation of an altered scorecard (1754); first disqualifica-

Reading the Green

tion for use of improper equipment (1754); first suspension for profanity (1754); first caddie fired for accepting a bribe (1754); first expulsion for throwing clubs (1754); first properly replaced divot (1897); first single permitted to play through (1924); first totally restored bunker surface following the play of a sand shot (1946); first completely honest handicap claim (1957); and first lost ball recovered by a following golfer and returned to its rightful owner (1984).

Rain	*See* 5TH & 15TH HOLES.
Reading the Green	Since greens are rarely level and their surfaces vary in smoothness or "speed" depending on how moist the grass is and how recently it was cut, golfers must examine them closely to determine which way and how far the ball will roll. Even the "friendliest"-looking green will have some tricks up its sleeve, and many are downright hostile. Thus the "message" of any given green, as read by the well-trained eye of a seasoned player, can range from "Aim a little to the left" or "Look out—anything more than a light tap will run right by the hole" to "The best thing you can do with that putter is make it into a decorative lamp base" or "You'll be lucky to four-putt, and by the way, those are absolutely the ugliest trousers I have ever seen."
Recovery Shot	Any shot whose primary purpose is to get the ball out of a hazard or away from an obstacle and back into playable position on the fairway. The most important thing to remember when playing recovery shots is not to be greedy. It's far easier to forget to include in your score a single short shot that put the ball into the middle of the fairway than to try to get away without counting a half-dozen duffs, caroms or ricochets.

Relaxation

In golf, perhaps more than in any other game, relaxation is essential. Any tension in a player's body is instantly transferred to the swing or the putting motion, and the results are invariably disastrous. Even a slightly taut muscle can misdirect the path of the clubhead, sending an expensive ball into the water. An unnecessarily stiffened joint can lead to the kind of jarring, ground-hitting stroke that causes cumulative shaft-related damage to costly clubs and can lead to possible bone injury as well. And an overly rigid grip could, paradoxically, cause a muscular twitch that might allow the club to slip from the fingers during the follow-through, perhaps maiming another player and triggering a ruinously expensive lawsuit. So for goodness sake, try to relax!

Rim

The edge of the hole. A ball that goes around the cup without falling in is said to have rimmed the hole, or to have ringed, skirted, lipped, lapped or looped it. It may also be said to have curled, circled or rolled around it, or to have done a tour, a circuit, a round trip, an orbit or a buttonhook. There are one or two terms for a ball actually going into the cup, but they are used so seldom that it seems like a waste of space to include them here.

Rough

Unmown, naturally wild area bordering the fairway and sometimes separating the fairway from the tee. There are three basic types of rough: low rough, a narrow strip of 6-inch-high grass where the ball may be easily playable; high or deep rough, where the ball may be lost and, even if found, may be obstructed or otherwise unplayable; and dark rough, where the ball may be eaten or stolen and used as an object of worship by primitive peoples.

Round	Eighteen holes of golf, played in their proper sequence, followed by one or more additional rounds at the 19th hole.
Rub of the Green	A phrase used in the rules of golf to describe a situation in which the flight of a ball is interrupted by anything other than another player in the match or his or her caddie or equipment. In such cases the match is continued and the ball is played from wherever it lands unless "whatever accidentally stopped or deflected the ball rattles, hisses, spits, growls or snarls; or stings, bites or drools; or makes menacing gestures or motions, or circles or makes ready to pounce; or has claws, fangs, a gun, a badge or a lawyer."
Rules	As currently constituted, the rules of golf consist of 34 basic regulations. The present record for breaking them in a single 18-hole round is an astonishing 31, with 69 penalty strokes, set in 1983 by J. Ward at Twittendon.

S

Sand Iron	A specially designed, deep-faced, heavy-soled iron club used to move a ball back and forth within a bunker or propel it out of one bunker and into another.
Sclaff	Onomatopoetic Scottish word for a muffed shot in which the ground is contacted before the ball is hit. The game's Caledonian inventors had plenty of time to develop a rich vocabulary for golfing mishaps, such as a ball topped lightly into the water (*firkel*), a ball hit a short distance through dense grass (*gleff*), straight into the air (*pooth*), into the woods (*slessgrack*), into rocks (*lofonnock*) and into other players (*yebastard*).

Scratch Player

Score	The total number of strokes needed to complete 18 holes or three times the caddie's tip, whichever is closest to 75.
Scorecard	A piece of paper on which a player's opening offer is written prior to the commencement of serious negotiations.
Scratch Player	A player with a handicap of zero; a par golfer; a rat; a louse; a stinker.
Senior	A golfer who attributes poor play to the fact that he or she lacks the physique of a younger player. *See* Junior.
Set of Clubs	A collection of no more than 14 golf clubs, usually consisting of three or four woods, nine or ten irons, and a putter. The chief distinction among the types of clubs is that the woods make a sound like "sneck" or "frop" when the ball is improperly hit, whereas the irons emit a sharp "jink," "fank" or "whenng" and the putter produces a soft "tilk."
Shag	To retrieve golf balls. Golf is full of odd terms and expressions. After hitting a 5-iron shot right onto the green, for example, you might answer an opponent's question about what club you used by saying, "The *stick* I used was a 7-iron"; when citing a nonexistent rule to improve your lie, you might say, "I'm claiming *relief* from this lie under the rule covering tassleclots"; and after scoring a 6 on a hole, the right way to report your tally is to say, "I *carded* a five."
Shank	The most dramatic and unsettling form of misplayed shot, in which, as the clubshaft vibrates violently, the ball flies off to the right at nearly a 90° angle, embarrassing the golfer and endangering his or her fellow players. Duffers who consistently shank their balls are urged to buy and study *Shanks—No Thanks* by R. K. Hoffman or, in extreme cases, M. S. Howard's excellent *Tennis for Beginners*.

Short Game
The short shots played around the green (chips, putts, pitches and sand trap blasts) and the cheap shots taken between the green and the next tee (quips, digs, cracks and jests).

Skull
To hit the upper part of the ball, causing a fast, low driving shot. You might try hitting slightly more under the ball with a sweeping movement of the arms.

Sky
To hit too far under the ball, causing a high, ballooning shot. You might try using your hands to open up the clubface a bit.

Slice
To hit the ball with too open a clubface. You might try closing it up a little.

Smother
To hit the ball with too closed a clubface. You might try opening it back up and hitting more on the upper part of the ball.

Sock
To hit someone under the chin or on the lower part of the face with a closed hand driven by a fast, upward-sweeping movement of the arm.

Spin
Professional golfers and other accomplished players can apply a variety of spins to the ball to make it curve around obstacles, turn into the wind or stop dead where it lands. These shots take skill and practice, but most beginners have a bag of tricks, too! For example, even the rankest of amateurs can amaze their playing companions and themselves by making a ball run right across the centre of the hole without going in, rise straight up into the air, execute unbelievably sharp left or right turns, travel sideways or even backwards, or disappear entirely.

Stance	The proper positioning of the feet for the golf stroke may seem a fairly complex matter, but there are really only a few basics to master: just remember to put the clubhead behind the ball with your left hand on the grip (some say the right hand), then step forward with your right foot (some say the left foot), bring up your left foot (or right) and grasp the grip with your right hand (or left). Now line up the ball with your left heel, your left toe, the inside of your left foot, or between your feet, with the left foot slightly forward, the right foot slightly forward, or both feet parallel. That's all there is to it!
Straitjacket	Confining garment that some golfers have found to be necessary after long periods spent attempting to master the stance.
Stroke	Any forward movement of the club that is made with the intention of hitting and moving the ball and is observed by another golfer.
Stymie	A ball whose path to the hole is blocked by another ball is said to be "stymied," and under current rules the impeding ball is marked and moved. At one time, such shots had to be played by making the ball hop over or curve around the impediment, but a notorious, deliberately laid stymie during extra holes of the 1951 English Amateur Championship led to a modification of the rule, first in Britain and then, a little later, in the U.S. Other important rule changes and the circumstances under which they were made: LIMIT SET ON TIME SPENT SEARCHING FOR LOST BALL: "The Lang, Lang Combing of the Glen," 14th hole, Loath Links, October 11, 1871–April 8, 1872

Stymie

Swing

UNORTHODOX SWINGS AND CLUBS DISALLOWED: Lacrosse player François Foisette wins the Canadian Open, 1899

"ELIGIBLE PLAYER" MORE FULLY DEFINED: Kabu, a chimpanzee, wins the Calcutta Open, 1901

PLAY STRICTLY PROHIBITED FROM LIES BEYOND THE BOUNDARY OF A COURSE: "The Mashie Incident," British-Chinese border skirmish, Hong Kong, 1909

FOURTEEN-CLUB MAXIMUM ESTABLISHED: "Relatively Bloody Saturday," the Caddie Strike of 1926

DISCONTINUANCE OF TOURNAMENT PLAY PERMITTED: "The Battle of the Glorious Leg-of-the-Dog 15th," third round of the Spanish Open, Valencia, 1937

BALL REMOVED FROM COURSE BY DOG DECLARED UNPLAYABLE: R.S.P.C.A. v. Royal and Ancient Club, 1948

NO PENALTY FOR ACCIDENTALLY KNOCKING BALL OFF TEE: Executive Order Number 1, President Gerald Ford, 1974

Sudden Death	Term for the situation that exists when a match is tied at the end of 18 holes and the player who feels the least amount of confidence about beating the opposition in extra-holes play suddenly remembers the death, earlier in the day, of a beloved aunt.
Swing	A full golf swing consists of the backswing that carries the clubhead up to the topswing point, the downswing that brings the clubhead to the point of impact, and the follow-through. If the ball dribbles a few feet forward or hooks or slices violently into the woods or rough, the follow-through can be extended into the foresling—a graceful, lateral motion that sends the club spiraling into the undergrowth. Alternatively, the follow-through may be stopped and the club brought up sharply in a vertical arc until the clubhead is behind the back, pointing at the ground, then swept

smoothly up into the more classic topfling, which combines the power and accuracy necessary to send even the heaviest club into a distant water hazard.

T

Take-away	The initial part of the backswing. The name derives from the fact that a properly executed, ground-scraping, slow, backward sweep of the club with the clubhead pressed firmly onto the ground will "take away" most impediments interfering with the lie.
Tap-in	A putt short enough to miss one-handed.
Target Line	An imaginary line from a player's lie to the target which the ball would follow if an imaginary golfer hit it.
Tee	Small wooden peg on which the ball is placed for a drive from the teeing ground. The condition of the tee after the tee shot provides an indication of whether or not the ball was hit correctly. If the tee flips backwards and lands in one piece a few inches behind the place where it was inserted into the grass, the ball was probably hit well. If, on the other hand, the tee breaks into three or more pieces, is driven deeper than two inches into the ground, travels farther than the ball or catches fire, it probably wasn't.
Tee Off	To drive a ball off a tee. Players who have made their drives off a tee are said to *have* teed off, but at this point it is almost always also correct to say that they *are* teed off.
Teeing Ground	A clearly defined rectangular area 2 club-lengths in depth from which players hit shots 20 to 30 dub-lengths directly forward or 5 to 10 flub-lengths to either side.

Temper	*1.* Metal transformation into a heated state in which stiffness and strength are imparted to steel club shafts. *2.* Mental transformation into a heated state in which bends and crimps are imparted to steel club shafts.
Three!	What many golfers, through habit, cry instead of Fore!
Tight Lie	Poor playing position in which the ball is lying low in the grass or sitting on a bald or bare spot. Also known as a "close lie" or, more commonly, as an "original lie," "preliminary lie," "previous lie" or "former lie."
Timing	Precise control of the speed of movement in the swing to achieve the greatest possible power and accuracy. If a player's timing is off, then there is no way his or her shot will reach its...
Tip	A piece of advice, such as "You know, you need to work on your timing." ...intended target.
Top	To hit the ball well above its centreline, causing it to hop or trickle a few feet forward. Topping the ball is a problem that usually afflicts only beginning golfers, and it is quickly left behind once a player has learned to master the hook, the slice, the shank and the air shot.
Tournament	An elaborate, time-consuming but basically fair method used by many clubs to decide which individual members will be stuck for the next 12 months with the job of polishing, dusting and displaying their huge collection of ugly silver trophies.
Triple Bogey	Three strokes more than par. Four strokes more than par is a quadruple bogey, 5 more is a quintuple, 6 is a sextuple, 7 is a throwuple, 8 is a blowuple, and 9 is an ohshutuple.

Three

U

Umbrella

The only long, stick-shaped object with a shaft and a handle routinely found in golf bags that is just as useless in getting the ball into the hole as a putter is.

Unplayable Ball

The rules of golf make the player "the sole judge" of whether his or her ball is unplayable, and most players use this judicial power to waive the usual penalty for moving the ball in the light of their standing in the community.

Up and Down

Holing out from off the green in two strokes: an approach shot and a single putt. It is more common for players to go "up, across, beyond, next to, around and down" or "up, way over, under, into, through, along, onto, beside and down."

U.S.G.A.

The United States Golf Association, which acts as the rules-making body for the American version of golf, a fast-paced game played by two teams of 12 men each on motorized carts in large, indoor stadiums.

V

Vardon Grip

The almost universally used golf grip, in which the little finger of the right hand overlaps the forefinger of the left. Its invention is attributed to the legendary golfer Harry Vardon, a true innovator in the game who also developed an over-the-neck muzzlegrab for dislodging a ball from the jaws of a dog, a one-armed stranglehold for persuading recalcitrant golfers to recompute the totals on their scorecards, and a two-handed throatgrasp for throttling a caddie.

Water Hazard

W

Waggle
To swing the club back and forth in short, sweeping motions above the ball after addressing it and before beginning the backswing. Another preparatory motion players often make is a "forward press," a slight shifting of weight to the left leg accompanied by a partial bending of the right knee just prior to starting the backswing. In extreme cases, particularly when a crucial stroke is about to be made, players may, even before setting up for the shot, make an "upward address" by fully bending both knees until they touch the ground, then tilting the head forward and clasping the hands together, fingers fully interlocked.

Warm-up Exercises
Although golf is not as physically demanding as most other sports, it certainly doesn't hurt to loosen up one's muscles before a round. Here are a few simple exercises designed to get you ready for the day's play:
○ Hold out your arm, make a fist, and shake it back and forth, then open the fist, palm facing inward, extend the middle finger, and pump your hand up and down.
○ Kick at the ground, then stamp on it, first with your right foot, then with your left, then jump up and down.
○ Take off your hat, grasp it in your hand, throw it on the ground, pick it up, and repeat.
○ Raise your arms over your head, fists clenched, wave them vigorously and let out as loud a scream as you can, holding it for at least 15 seconds.

Water Hazard
Any boggle ub waddub borderburbled byb reb orb yellob markglubs fromble whidg idg uz legalble, bug ofteb inadvisabubble, tub tryb tub higgle thub ballablub.

Whiff	A stroke that completely missed the ball. The more prevalent term for this type of shot is "warm-up swing." *See* FLUFF.
Wind	Natural motion of the air. There are four basic winds that golfers have to contend with: a head wind; a wind that blows squarely in their faces; a wind that blows from the green towards the tee; and a wind that blows from a point directly in front of them to a point directly behind them.
Winter Rules	Local rules that permit balls to be lifted, cleaned and replaced in a preferred, i.e., more favourable lie without penalty during periods when adverse weather conditions make proper maintenance of the fairways impractical. Most golfers generally adhere to winter rules from the 1st of November until Hallowe'en.
Woods	*1.* Type of golf club used to drive the ball a long distance. *2.* Where the ball lands after being driven a long distance.
Wrist	In golfers, the swollen joint that connects a sore hand to an aching elbow and a painful shoulder.

X

X-outs	A series of Xs are printed over the brand name of some golf balls to indicate that, because of minor imperfections, they are "x-outs," or "seconds," and are cheaper than a properly manufactured ball. Golf balls are a lot less expensive than they were in the early days of the game, when the handmade, goosedown-stuffed, leather-covered "featherie" or the rubber "guttie" represented a sizable investment, but it can

still be painful to lose one. Thus, golfers who routinely fire balls into water hazards or the woods will, when confronting these hazards, switch to an x-out ball or, in descending order of value, a "range ball" (one purchased in bulk from a driving range), "smilie" (a ball with a deep cut in it), "filchie" (a ball taken from another golfer's bag) or "spuddie" (a small potato).

Y

Yard One of the basic units of measurement in golf. Some others are: the stroke (1.4 swings = 1 stroke); the minute spent looking for a lost ball (1,145 seconds); a 30-foot putt (divide by 5 if preceded by the phrase "I sank" and by 10 if preceded by the phrase "I missed"); the club-length in determining whether a putt is a gimme (the length of the clubhouse along its longest axis, not including stairs or porches); and liquid measure at the 19th hole (one drink = two drinks).

Z

Zero Also known as a hole-in-none, a score of naught on a hole is theoretically possible if an outside agency, such as a dog, should snatch the ball off the tee during a player's backswing, run with it to the green, and deposit it in the hole. No "O" has ever been entered on an official scorecard in Britain, but since formal record-keeping began in 1936, there have been 714 "nils" in Ireland.

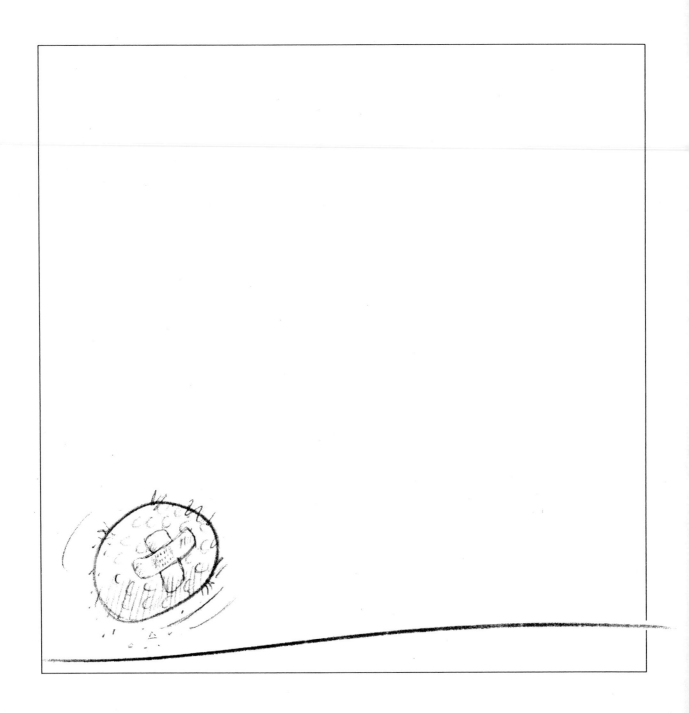